GIVE ME **ONE GOOD REASON** TO MISS ETERNAL LIFE

GIVE ME ONE GOOD REASON

To Miss Eternal Life

Dr. Bob Moorehead

Overlake Christian Press
Kirkland, Washington

Unless otherwise noted, the Bible version used in this publication is The Holy Bible: New International Version. Copyright © 1973, 1978, 1984 International Bible Society.

Overlake Christian Press
9051 132nd Avenue N.E., Kirkland, Washington 98033.

Printed in the United States of America.

ISBN 0-9639496-0-8

CONTENTS

INTRODUCTION

"Can you think of one good reason why you shouldn't buy this vacuum cleaner?" The good-looking young salesman was smiling but firm. He had demonstrated BEYOND question the merits of his product. It was a "state-of-the-art" cleaner in every way. It was light-weight, easy to store, and above all else, had tremendous suction power to pull dirt right up through the pad, through the carpet and into the bag! To be sure, we needed a cleaner. Our old one, which itself was a hand-me-down, had finally expired.

So, his question was certainly in line, and to his mind, he had covered everything, answered every objection, and had his order book in hand as he asked the above question..."Can you think of any reason...?" My response was simple, quick, and pragmatic. "NO MONEY." In spite of the easy payment plan he offered spread over three years, we still couldn't fit it into our budget. He disappointingly got his demonstration kit together, left us his card, and politely left saying he hoped we would change our minds, and if we did to be sure and call him.

I knew how he felt to a degree. I quickly recalled the many times I sat in someone's living room and shared the claims of Christ, the good news of the gospel, only to have the person say "no," or "not right now," or "I'll have to think this over." To be sure, my "product" was a far cry from a vacuum cleaner, and the "cost" of what I was presenting was zero, but still many people said "no."

When I have asked at that point, "Is there any reason why you SHOULDN'T accept Christ and commit your life to Him," I have received a plethora of excuses (often called reasons) why a person couldn't or wouldn't accept Christ.

Please note the inherent differences in the two "products" we're talking about.

1. One has a monetary price attached, the other is free.

2. One lasts for time, the other for eternity.

3. One is sold by human convincing, the other is given away by Holy Spirit conviction.

4. One will break or wear out, the other won't.

5. One will clean your carpet temporarily, the other will clean your soul for eternity.

6. One is made by man, and the other is made by God.

Maybe you are one to whom the claims and offer of Christ have been presented, and for one reason or another, you have deferred acceptance. You're not necessarily opposed to Christianity, the Bible, or the gospel, you just haven't accepted it into your own life for some reason.

Each of the chapters of this book deals with answers I've heard through the years when I've asked people to receive Christ as their Savior. As you read them, maybe you'll find the one you've used.

I came to Christ as a teen-age boy. It was, and continues to be, the most life-changing, convulsive, and revolutionary happening in my whole life. It brought hope in place of hopelessness, joy in place of despair, life

instead of death, and light instead of darkness. Because of Christ, I know where I'm
going in this life, and where I'll land in the
next! My prayer is that you will discover the
very same thing!

ONE

THE CLAIMS OF THE GOSPEL

The New Testament opens, as Mark has it, with these words;

> "The beginning of the gospel about Jesus Christ, the Son of God." (Mark 1:1)

Before you can say "YES" or "NO" to the claims of the gospel, you really need to know what the gospel is. The word "gospel" in the Greek language, the original language of the New Testament, really means "good news." Regardless of a person's station or rank in life, he must respond to this good news, yes or no. Many people have said "no" to the gospel, not because it wasn't worthy of saying "yes" to, but because it wasn't really the gospel they heard at all, but a facsimile of that gospel. They have heard, on the one hand, an aberrant version of the gospel that demanded a large amount of legalistic rules and regulations with no grace, no mercy, no compassion, and no love. On the other hand, they may have heard a distorted version of the gospel that preaches universal salvation; i.e., everybody is going to be saved just because they belong to the human race.

Both distortions are obviously wrong. So it is in scripture. Before anything can be good news, it must be contrasted against the backdrop of bad news first, or it isn't really good news. For example, if a doctor tells you that you have a deadly kind of cancer that will kill you in four to six months, and THEN tells you he has a serum that will destroy that cancer so that you can live, his good news is just that because it comes on the heels of the bad news about your health.

Before I get to the exciting good news of the gospel, let's first of all see why it is good news, by stating the bad news about mankind.

The Bible teaches the need for a good news gospel because man's nature is depraved, defiled, and sinful beyond hope of human repair.

Our common parents, Adam and Eve, sinned in the garden by eating of the forbidden fruit, and defiled their very natures in the process. Indeed the Bible teaches us that sin made its entry into this world through one man.

> "Therefore, just as sin entered the world through one man, and death through sin, and in this way death came to all men, because all sinned—..." (Romans 5:12)

In other words, once Adam was defiled (his nature made sinful), like produced like, and all his descendents became that way. In I Peter 1:18, Peter speaks of this "empty way of life" (our sinful nature) being handed down to us from our forefathers. Not only did that sin nature affect every part of our being, it was all pervasive with mankind. All became sinful.

"All have turned aside, they have together become corrupt; there is no one who does good, not even one." (Psalm 14:3)

That it was handed down generationally is alluded to again by David:

"Surely I was sinful at birth, sinful from the time my mother conceived me." (Psalm 51:5)

He traces his sinful problem all the way back to his conception. He was not only conceived in sin, but born in sin. He didn't have to do anything to become a sinner, he was a sinner from the time his father's sperm fertilized his mother's egg and he was conceived.

Therefore, we don't become sinners because we commit sins, but rather we commit sins because we are sinners.

Secondly, the consequences of that sin, if we do nothing about it, are monumental to say the least.

Separation From God
The first consequence is that we are sepa-

rated from a holy and righteous God.

> "But your iniquities have separated you from
> your God; your sins have hidden his face from
> you,..." (Isaiah 59:2)

The Bible teaches that God is a pure, holy God, and cannot co-exist with sin. Thus, sinful man is separated from God. Jeremiah also states that our sins separate us from the blessings of God as well.

In referring to the autumn and spring rains, as well as harvest he writes;

> "Your wrongdoings have kept these away,
> your sins have deprived you of good."
> (Jeremiah 5:25)

Sin Brings Wrath

No one talks much about the wrath of God anymore because it's unpopular. Yet the Bible is full of instances where God poured out His wrath in response to man's sin. The Bible also teaches that when we refuse to accept Christ, we incur God's wrath because we refuse to accept His remedy for our sin. Thus, sin brings wrath.

> "But because of your stubbornness and your unrepentant heart, you are storing up wrath against yourself for the day of God's wrath." (Romans 2:5)

Also;

> "...whoever rejects the Son will not see life, for God's wrath remains on him."(John 3:36b)

Sin Brings Spiritual Death

God told Adam he could not eat of the tree of the knowledge of good and evil, and the day he ate of that tree he would surely die. He wasn't talking about physical death, because Adam didn't die then, but of a spiritual death. When Adam disobeyed God, he began to die spiritually and passed that death on to his descendents.

The Bible says in Romans 6:23 that the wages of sin is DEATH, but the free gift of God is eternal life through Jesus Christ. Sin's consequences lead to a spiritual death and insensitivity to God that cannot change or be helped without the direct intervention of God. Ephesians 2 talks about man being dead in his trespasses and sins.

The consequences of sin are lethal and destructive. Sin left unaddressed by God's miraculous remedy, Jesus Christ, will also eventually take us to hell.

> "If anyone's name was not found written in the book of life he was thrown into the lake of fire." (Revelation 20:15)

The bad news about man gets worse when we realize that not only is his disease fatal, but man can do nothing about his sinful condition himself. It is beyond him.

> "The heart is deceitful above all things and BEYOND CURE. Who can understand it?" (Jeremiah 17:9)

Just as a dentist can't pull his own teeth, and a doctor can't remove his own appendix, so a sinner cannot save himself, or offer to God the price of his sins. When the above scripture says that man is beyond cure, it means his sinful condition cannot be cured by himself or any other person. The Bible says;

> "No man can redeem the life of another, or give to God a ransom for him—the ransom for a life is costly, no payment is ever enough..." (Psalm 49:7-8)

Paul reminds us in Romans 3:20 that no person can ever be saved by works or good deeds, or meritorious favors which he accomplishes. It takes divine intervention, though many people believe that because they are a good person they will surely be saved. Such delusion makes it very difficult for them to receive God's solution to their lethal problem, sin.

Biblically, sin is most often described as "missing the mark." It is failure to live up to a standard, and God's standard is perfection (Matthew 5:48). It's not what we DO that makes us sinners, it's that we are born sinners and are never able to live up to God's requirement, though many come close.

If you miss a flight by one minute and I miss it by one hour, which of us has missed it? Both, of course. Close doesn't count (except in horse shoes!).

Our culture has underestimated the devastating power of sin. Someone has said it well:

Sin will take you farther than you ever intended to stray.

Sin will keep you longer than you ever intended to stay.

Sin will cost you more than you ever intended to pay!

So, the bad news is out. We're all sinners (people who all have failed to hit God's target). Further, we can't do anything about our condition. It's not that we don't want to do anything about our sinfulness, it's that we're incapable.

Jeremiah was right when he wrote;

"Can the Ethiopian change his skin, or the leopard its spots? Neither can you do good who are accustomed to doing evil." (Jeremiah 13:23)

If all of that is true—that sin separates us from God, incurs God's wrath, and brings spiritual death and there's nothing we can do about it—it appears we're all doomed, right? Wrong! What man couldn't do, God has done. He has provided the serum, the antidote, the cure, if you please, for our sin. In His infinite wisdom, love and grace, God became man, for a little while, and paid the supreme price man could never pay, death on a Roman cross. Our acceptance by faith in God's divine and perfect solution removes the guilt and punishment of sin from us.

Since sin's just penalty is death, God, instead of changing His penalty, provided the person of Himself, manifested in Jesus Christ, to be the substitutionary sacrifice for the sin of ALL people of ALL AGES. While we were still in our sins and horrible guilt stood over our heads, God loved us and saved us;

> "...at just the right time, while we were still powerless, Christ died for the ungodly." (Romans 5:6)

When it says that Christ died FOR us, it doesn't just mean that his death was for our good, but that he actually died in our stead (place). Had God judged us only by the standard of justice, the sentence would have been crucifixion for all mankind. But the good news is that one died for all.

Again in Romans 5 Paul talks about the result of that one Man's act of righteousness, mankind's total and complete justification.

This is why the Bible teaches that we are saved by grace and not by our own good works. Grace is God giving us what we don't deserve. His mercy is withholding from us what we DO deserve. While on the cross, Jesus absorbed into Himself all the sin of all mankind for all time. In fact, the scripture says;

> "God made him who had no sin to be sin for us, so that in Him we might become the righteousness of God." (2 Corinthians 5:21)

In other words, Jesus got what He didn't deserve to get so that we can get what we don't deserve to get. He got the horrible penalty of sin, and actually "became" sin for us, and we got salvation, eternal life, and forgiveness of sin.

But while our "remedy" was provided when Jesus died on the cross and rose again from the grave, people don't just automatically get that remedy. They must opt to receive it by faith.

> "For it is by grace you have been saved THROUGH FAITH..." (Ephesians 2:8)

Saving faith is more than mere intellectual assent; that is, believing mentally that Jesus lived, died and rose again. Even the demons in hell believe that (James 2:19).

Saving faith is placing 100 percent of your trust in Jesus Christ alone for your salvation, and committing yourself to Him totally. You can say you trust a Boeing 747 to get you from Seattle to Seoul, Korea, but your trust becomes reality only after you board, sit down, fasten your belt, and allow the plane to take off. We can mentally believe a lot of things about Christ; in fact, everything the Bible tells us about Him. But until we commit ourselves to Him in that belief, we won't be saved.

How does that commitment come about? What does it involve on our part?

First, it involves repentance, a sorrow for sin that causes you to turn. The Greek word for repentance means to turn around and go in the opposite direction. Jesus said that unless we repent we will perish (Luke 13:3). The Bible says "now he commands all people everywhere to repent,"(Acts 17:30b). Repentance involves not only BEING sorry for sin, but telling God that you're sorry. It's being willing to say, "Lord Jesus, I am truly sorry for my sins."

Saving faith also leads us to confess Christ as Savior and Lord. The Bible says;

> "That if you confess with your mouth," 'Jesus is Lord,' and believe in your heart God raised him from the dead, you will be saved." (Romans 10:9)

Thus, our belief goes from our hearts to our lips, and proves we're not ashamed to be identified with Jesus and His saving act.

Are you willing to say YES to this gospel? You may, right now by verbally praying this prayer, preferably out loud.

> Dear God, I'm a sinner, and I'm sorry for my sin. I believe Jesus died for my sins and rose again on the third day. Lord Jesus, I receive You right now as my personal Savior and Lord. I repent of my sin and commit my life to You. Amen.

Did you pray it? If yes, welcome to God's forever family!

Please read on and help us remove the excuses that many use for not accepting Him and praying that prayer.

If you didn't, wouldn't, or couldn't pray that prayer, read on. Hopefully, by the time you're at the end of this book, you'll turn back to this page and settle your soul's eternity with God forever!

If you prayed the above prayer, and really meant what you prayed, there is some good news for you.

1. You are no longer under God's condemnation and wrath.

"Therefore, there is now no condemnation for those who are in Christ Jesus." (Romans 8:1)

2. You are a new person in the eyes of God!

"Therefore, if anyone is in Christ he is a new creation; the old has gone, the new has come!" (2 Corinthians 5:17)

3. You now have everlasting life with God!

"I tell you the truth, he who believes has everlasting life." (John 6:47)

4. You can be SURE of your eternal security!

"I write these things to you who believe in the name of the Son of God, so that you may know you have eternal life." (I John 5:13)

The good news about this gospel doesn't stop when you receive Christ. It goes on to say that no one can ever pluck you out of the Lord's hands (John 10:28-29).

T W O

"I'M NOT SURE THE BIBLE IS REALLY TRUE"

Kevin was obviously searching. He had visited our church two or three times. A graduate student in micro-biology at the university, he was hoping to pursue a teaching career someday. I was privileged to present to him the simple gospel delineated in chapter one. He listened intently as I told of the person of Jesus Christ being God's anointed Messiah, divine and human, and how He died on the cross to purchase with His own blood our salvation. I also shared with him how, through faith, he could receive the free gift of salvation.

He had no problem accepting man's sinfulness. Like all of us, he knew it first hand! He even had no problem basically believing in the existence of God, though he confessed he couldn't be 100 percent sure of that. The rub came when I finished the presentation. He said, "I wish I could believe what you're saying is all true, but because its credibility is based on the infallibility of the Bible I can't accept it, because I'm not sure the Bible is true.

As you read this, maybe this has been the hindrance keeping you from accepting Christ. The common stock objections range from, "Isn't the Bible full of contradictions and errors?" to "The Bible has been translated and copied so many times, hasn't this process led to errors?" Other objections always bring up the scientific reliability of the Bible, that somehow it is "out of synch" with modern science. Most critics of the Bible's accuracy have never read the Bible, or, at best, have read parts of it in a cursory way, looking for inconsistencies.

I often ask people, as I did Kevin, "What is the main message of the Bible?" Answers to that question range widely from a book of rules and regulations to how we can make this world a better place in which to live. I've discovered that most people reject the Bible, not even knowing or understanding what its main message is. Logically speaking, we can only reject something on the basis of what we know.

For example, I reject the doctrine of communism because I have read thoroughly the Communist Manifesto. To reject it, I must know it. The same is true of the Bible.

I asked Kevin this question: "The main message of the Bible is how man can be saved and have eternal life. Kevin, I know you reject the Bible, but what, in your opinion, does the Bible say about how we get eternal life and salvation?"

He didn't have a clue, and honestly so, because he had never really read the Bible, except in bits and pieces on sporadic occasions.

Biblical documents are utterly reliable. For example, existing Hebrew (Old Testament) texts are supplemented by the recently discovered Dead Sea Scrolls, the Septuagint, (a Third Century B.C. Greek translation of the Old Testament), the Targums, and the

Samaritan Pentateuch, plus the Talmud (writings and commentaries related to the Hebrew Scriptures).

The quantity of New Testament manuscripts is more than sufficient in ancient literature. There are more than 5000 Greek manuscripts and 8000 Latin manuscripts, plus about 1000 more in other languages.

Because the Bible continually refers to events in history, those events are verifiable. Their historicity and accuracy can be checked by external evidence.

For example, it's documented that we find a secular reference to Jesus in a letter written a little after 73 A.D. by a man in prison whose name was Mara Bar-Serapion. The letter compares the death of Pythagoras, Socrates, and Christ. Other secular contemporaries of Christ mention Him in history: Tacitus, Suetonius, Pliny the Younger, as well as Lucian. The Jewish Talmud also mentions Jesus a number of times.

The Bible was written by a diversity of 40 authors, over a time span of 1500 to 1800 years, and includes narratives, letters, poetry, prophecies, sermons, wisdom and literature. Although there are 66 distinct books in the Old and New Testaments, there is one theme: redemption of mankind.

But what about the inspiration of the Bible. That word means "God-breathed." In other words, the claim is that the Bible is not the word of man but the word of God. What, then, are the claims of scripture about itself?

When speaking of the Old Testament, Jesus said;

> "It is easier for heaven and earth to disappear than for the least stroke of a pen to drop out of the law." (Luke 16:17)

He also said;

> "...Scripture cannot be broken." (John 10:35)

Further, Paul claimed;

> "All scripture is God-breathed, and is useful for teaching, rebuking, correcting, and training in righteousness..." (2 Timothy 3:16)

Peter also affirmed this;

> "...no prophecy of scripture came about by the prophet's own interpretation. For prophecy never had its origin in the will of man, but men spoke from God as they were carried along by the Holy Spirit." (2 Peter 1:20b-21)

This tells us that scripture isn't of man, but of God. That's why it's called God's Word.

Another confirming truth about the reliability of scripture is fulfilled prophecy. No one yet has been able to refute the unanswerable argument of fulfilled prophecy. For example, some 300 Old Testament predictions were fulfilled inJesus Christ, in fact these messianic prophecies make no sense apart from His life. For example here are a few Old Testament prophecies made hundreds of years prior to the coming of Christ, and their corresponding fulfillment in the New Testament.

Old and New Testament Prophecies Fulfilled:

Birth at Bethlehem   Micah 5:1
                            Matthew 2:1

Born of Virgin	Isaiah 7:14
	Matthew 1:18-20
Riding a donkey	Zechariah 9:9
	Mark 11:1-10
Messiah suffering	Isaiah 53
	Acts 13:13ff
Messiah killed	Isaiah 53
	Acts 13:26ff
Messiah resurrected	Isaiah 53
	Acts 17:1-4
Messiah despised	Isaiah 53:3
	John 8:48ff
A lamb to slaughter	Isaiah 53:7-8
	Acts 8:30-35
Pierced hands & feet	Psalm 22:17
	John 19:18ff
Not a bone broken	Psalm 34:20
	John 19:33ff
Cast lots for clothes	Psalm 22:18
	Matthew 27:35
Cleansing of Temple	Psalm 69:9
	John 2:13ff
Died with transgressors	Isaiah 53:12b
	Mark 15:27-28

Those are but a few of the prophesies made. Nothing authenticates the authenticity of the Bible like this.

The most important part of the Bible is what it has to say about Christ. If Jesus is who the Bible claims He is, and if His claims are true, we have a big decision to make about Christ.

Josh McDowell's famous book, *Evidence that Demands a Verdict,* has well stated the principle. He begins with the supreme claim of Jesus. Jesus claimed to be God.

1. The Bible clearly says in John 1:1;

> "In the beginning was the Word, and the Word was with God, and the Word was God. He was with God in the beginning." (John 1:1-2)

Then John goes on to say of this Word;

> "The Word became flesh, and made His dwelling among us." (John 1:14)

It is clear from this that Jesus was not only the Son of God, but was God in the flesh.

2. Jesus Himself claimed to be none other

than God. In John 10:33, the Jews told
Jesus they were stoning Him because He
was claiming to be God! Jesus didn't deny
the claim.

In John 8:58, Jesus claimed to be God by
saying, "before Abraham was born, I AM."
This was equivalent to saying He was Yaweh
(Cf. Exodus 3:14). He also said to Phillip in
John 14:9, "anyone who has seen me has seen
the Father." He also accepted worship by
men (Matthew 18:20 and 28:20). He also
spoke of his sinlessness (John 8:46), claiming
power to forgive men's sins (Mark 2:5-11).

3. He also claimed to be the only way to God
(John 3:18, 8:24, and 14:6).

Josh McDowell cleverly presents for us a
process about Jesus.

He begins with Jesus claiming to be God.
There are two alternatives to that. Either the
claim was false, or the claim was true. If the
claim is FALSE, there are two alternatives:

He KNEW His claims were false, made a
deliberate misrepresentation, and was a liar,
hypocrite, a demon, and ultimately a fool, for

He died for it.

The other alternative of His claim being false was that He didn't know His claim was false, and thus was sincerely deluded and a lunatic!

Going back to the original two alternatives to His claim to be God, suppose His claim is TRUE? That means He is Lord. If He is Lord, there are two alternatives: Either you accept it or reject it. There are consequences to both. If His claim is in fact true, and history itself proves that it is (to say nothing of God's Word), and you accept it in your own life, you have life eternal with Him. If His claim is true and you REJECT it in your own life, you have everlasting life in Hell without Him. It's a clear choice.

I've often said to people who question the truthfulness and accuracy of the Bible: "If it's claims and Jesus' claims are all false, I haven't lost anything in eternity by believing it in this life. If it's claims are in fact TRUE, you have lost everything, not only in this life, but in eternity as well. I'd rather accept the Bible as true, and Jesus as Lord, wake up in eternity and find out it was all a lie, than to reject it all, and wake up in eternity and find out it was all TRUE."

When I put it that way to Kevin, he eventually came to the place where he willingly placed his faith in Jesus Christ, His death, burial, and resurrection from the dead. He's a strong Christian today. What about you?

THREE

"THERE ARE TOO MANY HYPOCRITES IN CHRISTIANITY"

When a person feels pressured to make a decision about Jesus Christ, and wants to say no, the easiest way to pull it off is to discredit the movement by the charge of hypocrisy.

And of course, it's true. One doesn't have to look far to find people who are inconsistent with their Christian walk.

But to discredit the validity of Christianity because of the inappropriate behavior and lifestyle of a few people who claim to embrace it is not reasonable. We wouldn't dream of "writing off" the police department of our city because there are a few dishonest policemen on the take. Nor would we dream of discrediting the whole United States Navy because we once knew a sailor who broke the rules.

It's interesting that Jesus told us in parable form that someone came and sowed weeds among the wheat. When the wheat sprouted, so did the weeds appear. When the owner was notified, he made it clear that an enemy had done this.

They were not to be pulled out just yet, but at harvest. Then they would be tied and burned and the wheat would be gathered into the barn (Matthew 13:24ff).

The application is clear. Not everyone who claims to be a Christian is one. In fact Jesus said, "Not everyone who says to me 'Lord, Lord,' will enter the kingdom of Heaven," (Matthew 7:21). In other words, profession doesn't mean possession. Just because someone claims to be a Christian doesn't mean he is a Christian. Just as art, money, and jewels can be counterfeited, so can Christianity. Just because counterfeit money exists doesn't mean we should stop using money! When money is counterfeited, it's because it is of value. Counterfeiters don't counterfeit pennies and one dollar bills, but 20's and 50's and 100's. If real Christians are counterfeited, it's because the real thing is valuable and truly precious.

The real question is not, "Are there hypocrites in Christianity?" The real question is, "Does the presence of hypocrites in Christianity invalidate it, and nullify the message of Christ?" Obviously, the answer is no. It is so easy to dredge up the worst travesties perpetrated in the name of Christianity. One could turn to the Salem witch trials, the Crusaders, or the Spanish Inquisition. They could also turn to the present and list exploitations, immorality, dishonesty, and other forms of unethical behavior. But to use these exceptional situations to discredit a whole movement doesn't make sense.

The word **HYPOCRISY** is taken from the Greek word "hupocritas," and described a Greek actor who put on another face during his stage performance, then took it off in his real life. The word has come to mean someone who pretends to be one thing, but in reality is something else; i.e., pretending to be something or someone he is not. When people pick out other people in the church and call them hypocrites, what they're really saying is that they are "pretending" to be Christians, but in reality they aren't.

Those who reject Christ on the basis of hypocrites may also be referring to people who are genuine Christians, but not perfect. Christians are **not** perfect, just forgiven! What would happen if I pointed to a less than perfect marriage, and said because she's not a perfect wife, and he's not a perfect husband, the institution of marriage isn't worth my time. The occasional inability to live up to the standard doesn't cancel the validity of Christianity. Besides, it's unfair to compare the life of one Christian with the life of another Christian and say he's not living up. It would be better to compare him to his life before he accepted Christ.

We wouldn't think of discrediting a particular diet that is guaranteed to enable people to lose weight by picking out the person on that diet who fell off of it, and is still overweight.

In the final analysis, Christianity stands on the person of Jesus Christ, not on the performance of Christians.

If you abhor hypocrisy, you are in good company. Jesus alone used the word "hypocrite" in the New Testament, holding His most severe words for those who practiced it.

In Matthew 23, He issued a stern series of woes to the religious leaders of His day because they had form without substance; or as some would say today, lots of merchandise in the display window, but their warehouse was empty! No less than six times, Jesus said, "Woe." He not only repeatedly called them hypocrites, He called them blind guides, fools, snakes, and whitewhashed tombs. To no sinner did Jesus ever say these things. You will not find one instance in the gospel accounts where during His lifetime Jesus ever condemned sinners. In fact, to the woman caught in adultery He said, "Neither do I condemn you." Not that He was soft on sin—He hated sin, but loved the sinner. He epitomized the hypocrisy of the religious leaders of the day by saying;

> "Woe to you, teachers of the law and Pharisees, you hypocrites! You are like whitewashed tombs, which look beautiful on the outside but on the inside are full of dead men's bones and everything unclean." (Matthew 23:27)

So, if you are down on hypocrisy, you're in good company!

Further, Paul described certain people as "having a form of godliness, but denying its power. Have nothing to do with them," (II Timothy 3:5). Such people obviously weren't true, authentic believers, but counterfeits, or he would never have urged us to have no fellowship with them.

Writing to Titus, he further said;

> "They claim to know God, but by their actions they deny Him." (Titus 1:16)

In discussing the anti-christ, John the apostle said this;

> "They went out from us, but they did not really belong to us. For if they had belonged to

us, they would have remained with us; but
their going showed that none of them belonged
to us."(I John 2:19)

By that statement, John certainly knew
there were pretenders. Their pretension was
confirmed by the fact that they didn't continue in the faith. In other words, they weren't
real and true Christians to begin with.

Not only is hypocrisy deplored in the New
Testament, Old Testament prophets constantly cried out against the empty front and
sham of Israel's worship and service. They
had the form, they said the words, they went
through the motions, but it was a surface
thing. Listen to one prophet's indictment:

> "I hate, I despise your religious feasts; I cannot
> stand your assemblies. Even though you bring
> me burnt offerings and grain offerings, I will not
> accept them. Though you bring choice fellowship
> offerings, I will have no regard for them. Away
> with the noise of your songs! I will not listen to
> the music of your harps." (Amos 5:21-23)

If you are not accepting Christ because of
hypocrisy in Christianity, please consider the
following:

1. The presence of hypocrisy in other areas of life doesn't keep you from acknowledging their credibility, so please don't select Christianity as the one area where you will allow hypocrites to keep you out of the kingdom.

2. Remember, there may be imperfect, weak, and mistake-prone people who are Christians, but don't mistake that for hypocrisy.

3. No doubt hypocrites are small people, but you would have to be smaller to hide behind them.

4. It isn't wise to allow another's behavior to determine **YOUR** eternal destiny. Romans 14:12 tells us that each of us shall give an account of OURSELVES, not someone else.

5. It's better to spend a few hours in church with a very few hypocrites than to spend eternity with ALL of them in the lake of burning sulphur (Revelation 21:8).

Therefore, remember that someday when you stand before God He will accept you on the basis of what you did with Christ here on earth, whether you accepted Him or rejected Him. He will not judge you on the basis of the behavior of someone else and how you reacted to it. Jesus Christ is the criterion by which we will all be measured.

> "In the past God overlooked such ignorance, but now he commands all people everywhere to repent. For he has set a day when he will judge the world with justice BY THE MAN he has appointed." (Acts 17:30-31a)

In the final analysis, it's your relationship with Christ that counts, not your reaction to a hypocrite. Why not turn back, right now, to the last page of Chapter 1 and pray that prayer, inviting Jesus Christ into your life. You'll be so glad you did.

FOUR

"I FEEL I'M GOOD ENOUGH THE WAY I AM"

I'll never forget Larry. Young, newly married, a good physique, clean cut, and holding down his first coaching job at the local junior high school. As I shared Christ, he very politely broke into the conversation to say, "Pastor, not to be disrespectful or rude, but I really don't feel I need to become a Christian. I live a very clean life, I don't lie, steal, cheat, swear, and I try to help other people, doing to them as I would have them do to me. I'm probably living a better life than most of your parishioners." I could tell by the tone of his voice and his general demeanor he was telling me the truth about his ethics and his moral life. If anyone was a paragon of clean living, it was Larry. As the evening wore on, he began to reason that surely God wouldn't keep him out of heaven, because he was basically a good person; not perfect, but close!

Maybe you feel the same way. Maybe ethically, morally, and in honesty, you're living a life of transparent integrity. Oh, you're not perfect, but by and large you're a good person; even other people say that about you. Because of this, you may feel no need of asking Christ to come into your life to be your Savior and Lord. Maybe you're like some people who use the ladder illustration. It's like putting the entire human race on a ladder; the better a person does and the more good deeds he does, the higher on the ladder he goes. Those who don't do so well are in the middle, and the murderers and rapists are at the lowest rungs. Of course, if you were to ask people on the ladder at what rung God will draw the line for salvation, most would say that it would be the rung JUST BELOW THEIR'S! This philosophy is bound up in the person who uses the phrase, "the best I can."

That somehow becomes God's standard, so it's a floating standard. One man's "best he can live" may be far lower or higher than another man's "best he can live." This position proposes that God really has no **one** standard for all, but a different one for different people. Of course, such a theology is foreign to the Bible.

If you are one who feels your good behavior (though not perfect) will somehow merit heaven for you, please consider the following problems.

1. Such a belief is predicated on the fact that God's anger against sin can be placated by good behavior. If bad behavior makes God angry, good behavior surely makes God happy with us. This is a "merit and works" approach. The more good work I can do the more chance I have of gaining heaven.

Of course, the Bible is clear about the fact that good works cannot gain us heaven.

> "Therefore no one will be declared righteous in his sight by observing the law;... (Romans 3:20)

"We who are Jews by birth and not 'Gentile sinners,' know that a man is not justified by observing the law,... because by observing the law no one will be justified." (Galatians 2:15-16)

"For it is by grace you have been saved, through faith—and this not from yourselves, it is the gift of God—not by works, so that no one can boast." (Ephesians 2:8-9)

"...he saved us, not because of righteous things we have done, but because of his mercy." (Titus 3:5)

The whole "works" for salvation is rooted in the idea of subtle pride. If we can merit or earn our salvation by what **WE** do, then in the end we get the glory. If our salvation is a gift of God that can't be worked for but only received by faith, then God gets all the glory. Dwight L. Moody once said that God saved us by grace and not by works because He didn't want to hear man crow in heaven for all eternity.

Believing that you're "good enough the way you are" assumes a floating standard of goodness. In fact, God has only one standard, and it's recorded in the Sermon on the Mount.

> "Be perfect, therefore, as your heavenly Father is perfect." (Matthew 5:48)

God has never changed His standard. It's still perfection.

"But," you respond, "no human being can reach that standard." You're right, no human being can become perfect on his own. Remember He said we must be as perfect as His Father who is in heaven. That's perfectly perfect! But of us the Bible says, "all have sinned and fall short..."(Romans 3:23). We fall short of perfection, some by a little, others by a lot.

If you lined all mankind up on one side of a cliff, and had as your object for them to jump 150 feet to the other side of the canyon, and each person could jump according to the degree of his sin, it would be an interesting thing. For example, the rapist and murderer would fall off the edge, jumping only about one foot. The thief might jump a little farther, say 10 feet. A very upright man like Larry, who was 80 percent perfect, would be able to jump 30 feet. What's happened? They have all jumped to their death, though some jumped farther than others! Even though there are differences of distances they were able to jump according to the level of their goodness, they all jumped to their deaths, because sin brings death, and salvation cannot be achieved by jumping.

Again, the book of James tells us all it takes to become imperfect.

> "For whoever keeps the whole law and yet stumbles at just one point is guilty of breaking all of it." (James 2:10)

God's justice demands that a penalty be paid for our sin and disobedience, our failure to live up to God's standard. While His justice demands payment, His love provides the price—the death of His Son, Jesus Christ. That alone can put us into a state of perfection in the eyes of God. God now looks at us through the blood of His Son, and that way He can see us as perfect.

2. If your good deeds can make you good enough to be accepted by God, then the death of Jesus Christ on the cross was the greatest mistake that has ever occurred in the history of mankind.

3. If you're actually saved by being good, then you, not God, have created the standard by which He accepts you.

It may "seem" reasonable and rational to us that this is the way God would do it, but remember what God said in Isaiah 55:

> "'For my thoughts are not your thoughts, neither are your ways my ways,' declares the Lord. 'As the heavens are higher than the earth, so are my ways higher than your ways and my thoughts than your thoughts.'" (Isaiah 55:8-9)

If you have to make a choice between what seems reasonable to us and what God says, we better go with what God says.

Proverbs 14:12 reminds us that there is a way that **SEEMS** right to a man, but the end is the way of death. Don't be lulled into thinking your way is right.

4. No matter how good you are, since you're not perfect, you are under a curse until you accept Christ.

> "All who rely on observing the law are under a curse, for it is written: 'Cursed is everyone who does not continue to do EVERYTHING written in the Book of the Law.'" (Galatians 3:10)

That's astounding. It tells us just how good we have to be in order to be good enough to make it. We have to keep the whole law **perfectly**. If you're not doing that (and no one is), then you're not good enough to make it by being good.

Our reliance for salvation must be on Jesus Christ and His finished work on the cross and empty tomb. Anything short of that is inadequate.

It is because we were not good enough the way we were that God initiated the death, burial, and resurrection of Christ. As stated earlier, our standard is Christ, not the fact that our behavior or good works is better than someone else's.

It's not how much you sin or how little you sin that matters when you're outside of Christ—it's the fact that you are a sinner, and need a Savior. Why not acknowledge that you are a sinner, and need Christ right now. Why not invite Him into your life at this very moment?

Remember, God doesn't grade on the curve! He has a standard by which we get into His kingdom, and that standard is not "elastic." We can't stretch it to make it fit the way we "feel," or to make it fit what our culture says is right. What may "seem" reasonable to you can never be the standard, only what God's word really says. Remember;

> "There is a way that **seems** right to a man, but in the end it leads to death." (Proverbs 14:12)

Don't trust your feelings, trust the facts of God's Word. Let His Word be your criterion, and nothing less. If His Word says that we're not good enough, then we're not good enough. If His Word says we can never be good enough on our own, then we can never be good enough on our own!!

If you have thought you were good enough the way you were, and you feel God's convicting hand on your life right now, why not pray the following prayer of surrender?

Dear God, I'm at the end of myself right now. I know I'm not good enough the way I am, so I hereby trust in Your goodness and Your righteousness. Come into my heart, Lord Jesus; I receive You now as my Savior. Amen.

FIVE

"THERE ARE TOO MANY THINGS TO GIVE UP"

I had never met Tom, but had an appointment to see him at his dorm on the university campus. He had visited our church, and was in our area from the East Coast for his sophomore year in college. Tall, somewhat shy, but resolute, we met in the dorm lounge. Because of lack of privacy, we strolled out on the lawn and sat down. Our chit chat revealed that Tom was raised in a very liberal home where he was allowed to do basically what he wanted. From the close of his junior year in high school his life basically consisted of one round after another of drugs, alcohol, and sex. Living in a co-ed dorm, coupled with the permissive atmosphere of university life, it was obvious he was still involved in a "playboy"

world. He had come to church at the invitation of a Christian student he met in his
biology class, and fellow soccer mate. They
played on the same team.

I asked him if he knew if he was going to
heaven when he died, and his response way,
"I pretty well know I'm NOT going there."
I asked him if I could share some good news
with him, and it was affirmative. I basically
shared how we're all sinners, and what the
consequences of our sinfulness are without
Christ. I told him how he could receive
Christ and have a living relationship with
God, then asked if he would be willing to do
just that.

His response? "I can't do that...I feel like
there's just too much to give up to make that
step...and I'm not through sowing my wild
oats yet."

Admittedly, I wasn't totally ready for his
answer. I asked if we could meet again the
next week, and he agreed. During the next
six days I dug, thought, prayed, and gained
some insight into where Tom was coming
from.

We met again, and I was able to share with him some logical answers to his "reason" for not accepting Christ.

Maybe you find yourself inwardly saying the same thing; too much to give up, too much to sacrifice, it will mean the end of all my fun, and "I'm not sure I want to change my lifestyle that radically."

An answer like that implies some presupposed, yet incorrect assumptions:

1. Becoming a Christian Means a Life of Boredom.

Nothing could be farther from the truth. Jesus told a parable in Luke 15 about a young man who came to his father one day and asked for his inheritance early. Once he got it, he "split the scene" only to "squander his wealth." He lived a life of selfishness and indulgence until he was broke. He got a job as a swine feeder, and the husks of the swine food began to look good to him. Broke, tired, and lonely, he decided to risk going back home. Instead of his father waiting at the gate to give him a tongue-lashing and a beating, his father was waiting at the gate to welcome him home. He had the fatted calf killed and called for a party. He put the best robe on his back, the signet ring on his finger, and shoes on his feet. If there is one thing that stands out in that parable it's the fact that when we come home, life is anything but boring, dry, stale or placid. No, it's a party, a celebration, an event!

Becoming a Christian isn't the end of fun, excitement, a good time, or adventure. In reality, it's only the beginning. Jesus said;

> "...I have come that they may have life, and have it to the full." (John 10:10b)

That certainly doesn't sound like life in Christ is a bore, does it?

To say that there's too much to give up also implies something else:

2. Becoming a Christian is Measured in How Much we Give Up.

That negative concept of Christianity has turned many people off and away from getting near the real thing. Many think Christianity is a set of do's and don'ts...some kind of legalistic mold into which every convert must be poured...all saying the same thing, doing the same thing, and each with the identical code of conduct as the other, etc. Nothing could be farther from what the real thing is.

Many cults demand of their devotees that they dress alike, all earn the same amount of money, all live with the same essentials, all wear their hair one way, and all pray the same prayers. Other aberrant forms of Christianity have lists of what kind of amusement and entertainment their follows are permitted to attend, and in some cases how much money can be spent in a year on "fun." But authentic Christianity is a life of freedom in the Lord. Jesus said;

> "Then you will know the truth, and the truth will set you free." (John 8:32)

Jesus said,

> "So if the Son sets you free, you will be free indeed." (John 8:36)

Paul also wrote to the Galatians;

"It is for freedom that Christ has set us free."
(Galatians 5:1)

The Christian life is a life of incredible freedom, not bondage to rules, legalistic mandates, or laws of men.

Another assumption is implied when someone says there's too much to give up in becoming a Christian.

3. Somehow by "Giving Up Things" We Better Merit Salvation.

It may not be said, but is certainly implied. To become a Christian, we won't be accepted unless we give certain things up that we've been doing. Since we've already covered the fact that good works and deeds of kindness cannot merit our salvation, suffice it to say that no amount of giving up things, or taking on habits can grant us salvation. That is done only by the grace (free, unmerited favor and good will) of God.

4. Somehow the Authenticity of Our Salvation Can Be Measured in the Amount of Things We Give Up.

Of course, we know that statement isn't true, yet many think salvation can be measured by how many bad habits we give up when we get saved. In other words, the longer list of bad habits given up, the more likely is our salvation for real.

This is seen in a first-century incident at Corinth. Some new Christians felt it was morally wrong to eat meat that had been sacrificed to idols. Others felt it was all right. Who was right? Paul reminded them that an idol is nothing at all in the world. He also reminded them;

> "But food does not bring us near to God; we are no worse if we do not eat, and no better if we do." (I Corinthians 8:8)

However, he later said that because the other person's conscience is weak it can become defiled unless we're willing to give that habit up. Eating that meat wasn't wrong in and of itself, but since it was perceived to be wrong, Paul said give it up for the sake of the weaker brother.

If you have not accepted Christ as your personal Savior because you feel there is too much to give up, think about this: God never asks you to give up anything in your life that isn't in the way of your relationship with Him. Secondly, whatever activity you're involved in right now that can stand up under the pure search light of God never has to be abandoned. The only things that will go out of your life are those things that are inconsistent with a good relationship with the Lord. God will never ask you to "give up" anything in your life that is worth keeping. He's the giver of every good and perfect gift, and desires more than anything from you to be praised and glorified. If there's something in your life that is detrimental to that purpose He has for you, then of course, it ought to go.

Again, many get the cart before the horse. God doesn't want you to give up the things that need to go, then receive Christ. He wants you to receive Christ, and those things that are incompatible with His presence in your life will go. As you read these very lines, you may be stuck in some addiction, and you're afraid that when you accept Christ you won't be **able** give them up. But remember a child cannot do a lot of things **BEFORE** he's born, but will be able to do them later. The fact that you cannot straighten out your life now, before you're saved, is the important reason why you need to let Christ do it for you **AFTER** you're saved.

One of the prerequisites to accepting Christ is repentance. Repentance, as explained in chapter one, is first of all, experiencing a remorse and regret for sin. It involves a strong desire to turn and go in the other direction. Even the power to do that is provided by the Lord, and not us. But once we have truly repented of sin, we take on a new attitude toward those things we once did that were an offense to God.   Where once we looked forward to doing them and anticipated with glee the indulgence of the flesh, AFTER receiving Christ, thanks to God's Holy Spirit dwelling in us, we soon hate and deplore those things and find ourselves seeking to avoid them. No, that doesn't mean we won't slip on occasion, even more than once, but it does mean that once we've given our hearts to the Lord, that break with the past becomes much easier and possible.

Many times I hear people say, "I'm afraid I won't stay faithful, that I'll bail out, and return to the old life."

Let me give you some good news. "Staying faithful" is not your department, but God's. One of the greatest promises written in the Bible to Christians is this;

> "being confident of this, that he who began a good work in you will carry it on to completion until the day of Christ Jesus." (Philippians 1:6)

Wow! The Christ who saves you has promised to totally keep you! For how long? Till the day of Christ Jesus. That means till Christ returns to this earth. I would say that's long enough. That doesn't mean we're to shirk or be passive, we are still exhorted in scripture to be watchful, diligent, and faithful. But that commitment on our part is fueled by His power, not our's. We have been promised to be kept strong.

> "He will keep you strong to the end, so that you will be blameless on the day of our Lord Jesus Christ. God, who has called you into fellowship with his Son Jesus Christ our Lord, is faithful." (I Corinthians 1:8-9)

Whatever fear we have of breaking with the past or "giving up" the bad habits of the past fades into insignificance in the light of those kinds of promises.

I remember once being with a man who asked another man to receive Jesus Christ. The man asked came back with, "I don't know, there's a lot to give up if I do that." I was surprised at my friend's response. "You're right, there is a lot to give up:

We give up darkness for light,
We give up defeat for victory,
We give up guilt for innocence,
We give up bondage for freedom,
We give up condemnation for acceptance,
We give up hell for heaven,
We give up sinfulness for righteousness."

How true, how true. The final question is this. What can you think of that's in your life right now that's worth keeping you out of eternity with God forever?

"BUT WHAT ABOUT THE HEATHEN"

"I'm not sure I can trust a Christ who judges the heathen when they've never heard. It isn't fair."

Maybe you have never come to faith in Christ because this issue has loomed large in your thinking. Often the question is put like this; "Will God condemn those people who have never had a chance to hear the gospel?"

When you stop and think about it, there are only three alternatives to that question:

No, God will not judge those people;

Yes, God will judge those people unfairly; or

Yes, God will judge those people fairly.

Most who raise this objection insist that those who have never heard about Christ are innocent and should not, or will not, be judged. If God will judge them, He will either be fair or unfair. We must assume from what the scripture teaches that God's judgments are just and right.

> "Will not the Judge of the earth do right? (Genesis 18:25b)

Again, we're told in Job 34:12;

> "It is unthinkable that God would do wrong, that the Almighty would pervert justice." (Job 34:12)

On top of this, we're taught that God will definitely judge all the earth:

Isaiah 66:16 tells us; "The Lord will execute judgment upon all men." "ALL" means just that—"ALL." No one will be missed, whether they've heard the gospel or whether they haven't.

Again, we're told;

> "For he has set a day when he will judge the world with justice by the man he has appointed." (Acts 17:31)

God's judgment is based on the light people have. However He judges, he will not hold people accountable for something they absolutley cannot know. They are judged according to the revelation they have actually received, and the moral standard they've been given. Most people think that the heathen are completely ignorant about God, thus unaccountable. Romans 2:12 tells us;

> "All who sin apart from the law will perish apart from the law, and all who sin under the law will be judged by the law." (Romans 2:12)

That passage clearly teaches that we will be judged in the light of what we have the opportunity to know.

Romans 1:20 talks about the outward (external) revelation of God to man.

> "For since the creation of the world, God's invisible qualities—his eternal power and divine nature—have been clearly seen, being understood from what has been made, so that men are without excuse." (Romans 1:20)

This is known as the "general" revelation of God, and even if people have never heard anyone preach about God, He has provided this way where He can be seen. Psalm 19 also shows that God has revealed Himself in nature;

> "The heavens declare the glory of God; the skies proclaim the work of his hands." (Psalm 19:1)

But there is also INTERNAL revelation. Romans 1:19 says;

> "since what can be known about God is plain to them, because God has made it plain to them." (Romans 1:19)

Though mankind is in a fallen state, it was made in the image of God with the latent capability of recognizing God.

Ecclesiastes 3:11 says that God has set "eternity in his heart."

Someone has wisely said that if man rejects the light he has been given, be it small, God will not give him further light. When we're obedient to the light we have received, then God gives more light.

Somehow it has been falsely alleged that a person who has never heard about Christ from a missionary or evangelist is safe because he is innocent. Let it be understood that no human being on earth is innocent.

> "God looks down from heaven on the sons of men to see if there are any who understand, any who seek God. Everyone has turned away, they have together become corrupt; there is no one who does good, not even one." (Psalm 53:2-3)

It's amazing how many times that same truth is presented in the book of Psalms. Paul said it clearly in the New Testament;

> "for all have sinned and fall short of the glory of God," (Romans 3:23)

Christ died for the WHOLE world, not just the ones who would hear the gospel. Everyone is responsible for his sin also, not just the ones who are fortunate enough to hear the good news. If Christ died for them, it's safe to presume that He will find a way to get that salvation message to those people,

either through a missionary, by general outward revelation, or by inward revelation.

Some are concerned about those who
lived before Christ...what happens to them?
The basis of every person's salvation, before
and after Christ, has been His atoning, sacrificial death on the cross. God saw the saving
work of Christ hundreds of years before it
occurred. Not limited to a time frame, God
provided the benefits of Christ's death and
resurrection to ALL who call upon him. This
means salvation has always been by faith,
never by works. The blood of the animal
sacrifices was powerless to save in and of
itself, but pointed ahead as a type to the Blood
of Christ who was to come. We're told in the
book of Hebrews that Jesus' sacrifice on the
cross wasn't just for those living during His
death and after;

> "But when this priest had offered for **ALL
> TIME** one sacrifice for sins, he sat down at the
> right hand of God." (Hebrews 10:12)

Many have been the occasion when I've
shared the gospel with people, only to have

them say, "Well, what about the African natives who have never heard about Christ. What's going to happen to them?" And though the Bible addresses that issue as we have seen, my stock answer to these folks in love is, "My concern right now is not the native in Africa five thousand miles away who has never heard about Christ, but about you right here and now who HAVE heard." Knowledge brings responsibility. The issue is acting on what we DO know, not on what the heathen do NOT know.

Remember, we are called upon in scripture to "go and make disciples of all nations." Five times in Matthew, Mark, Luke, John, and Acts, we're commanded to go to the nations and preach the gospel. There is a sense of urgency to do that, no one will deny. If God planned for all the heathen in those nations to be saved whether we go or not, His command is somewhat redundant. The presence of the command presupposes He will judge those people who never get to hear—maybe in a slightly different way, but He will judge them.

As you read these lines, you are more than likely not one of the heathen who has never heard. (If you've read this far in this book, you've heard!)

I leave you with this verse;

> "Anyone, then, who knows the good he ought to do, and doesn't do it, sins." (James 4:17)

To not know for us is one thing, but to know, and not act upon what we know is quite another. Knowledge demands decision. If a doctor tells me I have a fatal disease, then gives me the good news that he has a serum that can cure that disease, then I must make a choice. The choice is very simple. I either choose to do NOTHING, and die, or I choose to receive his serum and live. There really is no "third" alternative.

We all have a disease, it's called sin. God has the serum in Jesus Christ. We can either accept His serum or reject Him.

The choice is totally our's, but we must make the choice. Right after I moved to Seattle, there was a terrible fire in a hotel downtown. If I recall, there were three people killed in that fire. One man was needlessly killed. He was on the fourth floor, the firemen rigged a safety net and yelled for him to jump. They pleaded with him to jump. They begged him to jump. They assured him of its safety by going up on a ladder and jumping. As he sat crouched on the window ledge, the crowd below got into the act, shouting for him to go ahead, and that it was safe. As the fire spread and the smoke increased, he was overcome and fell backward into his room where he suffocated to death. The provision for life was there, but he opted for death out of fear.

Remember, Jesus put it this way;

> "...if you do not believe that I am the one I claim to be, you will indeed die in your sins." (John 8:24b)

So, the issue really isn't "What will happen to the heathen who never hear the gospel?" but rather, "What will happen to you who HAVE heard the gospel?" If you're still reading this, fortunately, there is still time! Why not turn to the back of chapter four and pray that prayer RIGHT NOW! Then you can join all the rest of us in seeing that the heathen hear this good news!

"I'M AFRAID I WON'T STAY FAITHFUL"

My chicken salad lunch had hardly been touched. You can't eat and talk at the same time. Carl and I had been in that booth for almost two hours. A computer programmer, he thought with a systematic precision that drives non-programmers crazy!

We had finished going over God's great plan of salvation, and precisely how he could receive that free gift of salvation. When I was about to take my second bite of the salad, and he was finishing his pie, he calmly said, "But I know me, and I have serious doubts as to whether I would stay faithful with this thing..." To "back up" his objection, he humbly confessed to me that he had started a strenuous diet on January 2, but "fell off" by Super-

Bowl Sunday! He also showed me his membership card to a health club for which he paid a
handsome $54 per month, and after working
out only a couple of weeks at the most, he had
never returned. He also invited me to ask Linda,
his wife, about the deck he had begun two years
earlier. He got the foundation partly in, but the
lumber had turned brown from the weather by
now, and he doubted that he would ever finish.
"I'm just not a finisher," he went on to say, "so
what's to say I'll stick with this?" (referring to
the Christian life).

It became evident that Carl was viewing my
invitation to receive Christ as some kind of
"club" or "organization" he was joining, and
that he just might lose interest in the "meetings"
or the "teachings" and drop out.

A common fear attached with becoming a
Christian is the fear that the commitment one
makes may not be lived up to in time, and then
that person would be worse off than he would
be had he never made the commitment. In other
words, it has been put to me this way; "It's
better NOT to do it, than to do it and not really
mean it."

It may well be that you have never made a commitment to Christ, because you're afraid you may "bail out" later when other interests come into your life. Such reasoning is often predicated upon some myths that seem easy to believe as true.

MYTH #1: It's up to us to stay faithful in our relationship with Jesus.

Without diminishing our personal responsibility as a Christian, let me be quick to say that if you're worried about "sticking with it" you need to worry no more. That's God's department! When you accept Christ, there are certain promises made to you by the Lord. One of those promises is that He will keep you.

> "I give them eternal life, and they shall never perish; no one can snatch them out of my hand. My Father, who has given them to me, is greater than all; no one can snatch them out of my Father's hand." (John 10:28-29)

These words of Jesus are more than just words. They are His personal guarantee that

He will not allow us to be "snatched" away by anything, including our faithlessness.

Again, we're told by the apostle Paul;

> "being confident of this, that he who began a good work in you will carry it on to completion until the day of Christ Jesus." (Philippians 1:6)

What God begins, He finishes. If you surrender your life to the Lord, He has promised to COMPLETE the work He begins in you. "But what if I lose interest and become faithless?" Please note, the passage above didn't say He will carry it on only IF YOU STAY FAITHFUL. Every Christian goes through varying degrees of faithfulness and unfaithfulness, but through it all, our position in Christ isn't affected.

One of the most powerful promises for every believer, especially a new believer, is found in I Corinthians.

> "He will keep you strong to the end, so that you will be blameless on the day of our Lord Jesus Christ. God, who has called you into fellowship with his Son Jesus Christ our Lord, is faithful." (I Corinthians 1:8-9)

Once again, we see the reaffirmation of God's faithfulness in this new relationship. He remains faithful to keep us. In fact, Paul wrote young Timothy these words;

> "If we are faithless, he will remain faithful, for he cannot disown himself." (2 Timothy 2:13)

Paul wrote to the Thessalonians;

> "The one who calls you is faithful, and he will do it." (I Thessalonians 5:24)

So the first myth is that somehow the continuation of our salvation is based on OUR faithfulness to God. No, it's based on God's unswerving faithfulness to us.

MYTH # 2: The Christian life consists of keeping rules and placating God with our good works.

When a person says he cannot accept Christ and become a Christian because he may not stay faithful is presupposing somehow that what he's "buying into" is only a worrisome obligation of performance on which he will be graded.

To be sure we have an obligation as a Christian to live the Christian life, but the primary function of a Christian is to develop an intimate relationship with the Lord, **not** just fulfill obligations for the Lord. Whatever obligations we fulfill are things which flow out of our close relationship with and love for Him. Jesus said, "If you LOVE me you will keep my commandments," not, "if you **fear** me." (John 14:23)

So if you're worried that you won't stay faithful, just remember that you are entering a relationship, not a bondage obligation contract!

MYTH # 3: The power to stay faithful is limited to human motivation.

In other words, many believe they may not stay faithful to Christ, because, like Carl, they haven't stayed faithful to much else in their life. This presupposes that we have available the same resource AFTER we accept Christ as we had BEFORE we accepted Christ. This myth has kept many people from surrendering their lives, I'm afraid.

The opposite, however, is true. Once we receive Christ, not only does the Lord stay faithful to us, He grants us the wherewithal to stay faithful to Him. Our faithfulness, then doesn't come from the storehouse of OUR power supply, but His.

We tend to forget that something revolutionary and radical occurs when we become saved. It's nothing short of this.

> "I have been crucified with Christ, and I no longer live, but CHRIST LIVES IN ME." (Galatians 2:20a)

Whatever my degree of faithfulness to the Lord may be as a Christian, it's Christ living in me that does it, not me.

I really think that is why Paul said;

> "I can do EVERYTHING through him who gives me strength." (Philippians 4:13)

Note: Paul didn't just say, "I can do everything." He added, "through him who gives me strength."

That's why as a non-Christian, we cannot say how faithful we think we will be as a Christian, because we don't have the super-natural resource in us now that we will have then!

MYTH #4:   No one should do anything if the possibility of failure remotely exists!

I'm glad Columbus didn't believe that myth. I'm glad Dr. Salk didn't believe that myth when he attempted to create a vaccine against polio. I'm glad Edison didn't believe that myth when he labored tirelessly on the light bulb. I'm glad my mother didn't believe that myth when she found out she was preg-nant with me!

People who say, "I'm afraid I may not remain faithful," don't say that about a new job, or a spouse when they get married, or about a project around the house. So why should we suddenly get cold feet when it comes to becoming a Christian?

In other words, some will launch out on some things, even in areas where they are not promised extra inner resources, but not into

Christianity where they are promised staying power.

The "risk" of not accepting Christ and spending eternity without God is so much greater than the "risk" of accepting Christ and not remaining faithful.

This discussion in no way minimizes our personal, spiritual responsibility to be faithful to Christ once we receive him. The Bible talks much about being "faithful until the end." What is important at this point is to understand how that faithfulness comes about. We can't create it, make it, or in any way contrive it ourselves. Our source for staying faithful is found in the Lord Himself. Truly, "we are more than conquerors through Him who loved us," (Romans 8:37).

Most importantly, remember the promise of God;

> "Never will I leave you; never will I forsake you." (Hebrews 13:5b)

Remember;

> "...I know whom I have believed, and am convinced that he is able to guard what I have

entrusted to him for that day." (2 Timothy 1:12b)

I firmly believe if we are truly saved, we will want to be faithful—it will be the over-whelming desire of our lives. God will honor that desire, because it will bring glory to Him.

The bottom line is this. It would be a tragedy indeed to stand before the great white throne judgment bar of God and hear God ask, "Did you ever receive my Son?" What if you had to answer, "No...," then you heard God say, "Why didn't you go for it, and I would have seen to it that you would have never bailed out." Then it will be too late. But there's still time now. How about it? Won't you invite Jesus Christ into your life right now?

EIGHT

"RELIGION WAS FORCED ON ME AS A CHILD"

I'll call them Keith and Jean. They had visited our church on two occasions, and I drew their name for calling one Tuesday evening. I decided to call before I went just to make sure it was all right for me to come. Keith was polite, but a bit stern as he said, "It's fine for you to come, but we won't tolerate any pressure." After some chit-chat, I made the mistake of asking them about their church background.

Keith became almost livid. "We're not Christians today because we were forced to attend church when we were small." Jean chimed right in. They both told of parents who went to church every time the doors were open, and sometimes when they weren't. They both told of how they were required to go and sit through hell-fire and damnation sermons. When both were in their late teens, they bade farewell to the church, rejecting what they called an "inordinate" strictness they never wished to impose on their family.

A young couple now in their late twenties, Jean and Keith had two children of their own. Those children were the reason they had very cautiously visited our church. They were feeling what most parents feel—an overwhelming sense that now with children, they need help. So I at least knew that under their tirade against what they called the "organized church," they were searching.

Keith and Jean had not accepted Christ into their lives because of their bad experiences in childhood. I asked for permission to share the gospel story, and they reluctantly allowed me to do just that. When I was through, I asked them if they would invite Christ into their lives. They both said no because relgion was "forced" on them as a child, and that if they ever decided to do that, it would be their decision and their's alone.

What I shared with them that evening and two subsequent visits, I share in this chapter.

You may be one of those persons who was forced to go to church as a child, and you want no part of it now. I think I might have some good news for you that will free you from that bondage.

The first response deals with respect. I said to the aforementioned couple that instead of bitterness they ought to respect their parents for attempting to do the right thing for them spiritually. No parent is able to raise children perfectly in all the aspects of their lives. Child-rearing is not something the university prepares you for, and no manual gives complete instructions. So though your parents made some mistakes in their attempt to provide the spiritual direction needed for your life, at least give them credit for trying. They may not have prepared you mentally for your life, but you don't repudiate all schools and universities because of that. They may have erred in teaching you true patriotism, yet you don't denounce your citizenship. They probably made some mammoth mistakes in their approach to disciplining you, but you obviously won't throw all discipline out and allow your child to be raised without any discipline at all. Guess what? You won't do a perfect job in raising your children, but hopefully they will give you credit for trying.

I also shared with Jean and Keith something else. There were other things your parents forced you to do when you were a child that were for your benefit...things you may not have liked at the time, but for which you are thankful today. I thought my mom was cruel marching me off to the dentist where, in those days, teeth were filled without Novocain! Though painful at the time, I'm glad now, since otherwise I would have no teeth.

Many were the mornings I was marched off to school over my protest. I'm sure glad now my parents put their foot down and "forced" me to go, or I wouldn't be writing this book.

I'm glad my mother "forced" me to eat the right kind of food as a child, or I would have overdosed on sweets. In retrospect, I'm glad my dad made me get a job when I was fourteen. At the time, I thought I had received the sentence of death. He was trying to teach me responsibility, though at the time I thought he was strategizing for one less mouth to feed by killing me! That taught me a discipline and responsibility that eventually got me through nine years of college and graduate school. I could have said as an adult, "I was forced to go to work as a child, so I will never work again." My first job was as a stock boy in a grocery store, so if I followed that reasoning, I might say, "I will never patronize a grocery store again."

So, since we don't stop shopping, learning, eating right, and going the dentist and doctor just because we were forced to as a child, why should we stop going to church, although forced to go as a child?

I also shared with Jean and Keith something I think they had forgotten. A bad experience with something doesn't automatically invalidate a thing. Because I get a lemon of a car at a disreputable dealer doesn't mean I'll never buy a car again. I will be more careful. Just because I bring home a gallon of milk that is a bit sour doesn't mean I'll never go to a grocery store again. Just because I buy a refrigerator that is defective doesn't invalidate refrigerators for me so that I go back to the old ice-box system, ordering ice twice a week. Just because there is a blemish in a new suit I buy doesn't mean I'm off of suits the rest of my life.

People can have a bad experience in a church. They often do. A person may visit a dead church, an unfriendly church, or an unbalanced church, but that one church certainly isn't representative of all churches. It is illogical to write off Christianity and its merits because a few of its representatives make some mistakes, or don't live up to your expectations.

Stop and think about one more thing. Does the fact that your parents forced you to be exposed to spiritual things as a child in any way justify your refusal of something that will affect all of your eternity? Remember, we're not talking about something that will affect you only during this earthly life, but something that will have a bearing on your whole eternity. I would never blame my parents for my being kept out of heaven. It's an individual choice.

The excuse of being forced to go to church as a child against your will for not accepting Christ now really can't hold much water. It's a poor exchange for missing heaven.

Look at your early childhood another way. It would be appropriate to thank your parents for at least making an attempt to raise you right. Thank them for caring enough about you to expose you to God, the Bible, the Church, and other Christian people. They may not have done it all right, but at least they made an honest attempt.

Regardless of what you were "forced" to do as a child in the spiritual sense, there is a truth that remains unchanged. It's the truth that we were all born with a sin nature upon us. We are totally incapable of doing anything to remove that nature. The Bible clearly teaches that until that sin nature is removed, God cannot accept us. In the fullness of time, God sent us Jesus who died on the cross and provided the serum for our sin. When we

accept Him, then we have reconciliation to
God. Those truths don't change.

If your refusal to accept Christ right now
as your Savior is due to the fact that you were
forced to go to church as a child, or you feel
you really got your "belly" full of "religion"
as a child, think about this: Our spiritual
roots go back to the Old Testament to Juda-
ism. God made it clear to parents what they
were to do with their children spiritually;

> "These commandments that I give you today
> are to be upon your hearts. Impress them on
> your **children**. Talk about them when you sit
> at home and when you walk along the road,
> when you lie down and when you get up. Tie
> them as symbols on your hands, and bind them
> on your foreheads. Write them on the
> doorframes of your houses and on your gates."
> (Deuteronomy 6:6-9)

Stacked against family life today and the
emphasis that is placed on the spiritual in-
struction in the home, the above command
sounds pretty radical, wouldn't you say? The
Hebrew word for "impress" used in the verses
above means to "weave something into some-

thing else." In other words, parents are commanded to do far more than make a passing occasional mention of spiritual things to their children. They are to make a deliberate attempt to teach their children the commands of God. If you feel your parents shoved too much teaching down your throat, at least give them credit for obeying what the Bible says. The fact is that some of the principles by which you live, and some of the principles you are weaving into the life of your children were given to you by your parents.

I'm glad to say that eventually Keith and Jean turned their lives over to Christ. They later confessed that for them and their children, their excuse could never hold water. If you have struggled with this issue in your life, why don't you do yourself and your parents a favor by humbling yourself before God, and asking Christ to come into your heart?

You might want to pray the following prayer:

> Lord Jesus, I thank you for the early training my parents gave me, though at times I have

resented that. Come into my heart right now,
I receive you as my personal Savior. AMEN.

Everyone reading this falls into one of the
following categories:

First you may be a parent yourself. If your
children are still in your household, you have
an awesome responsibility to guide their **spiritual** life so they will choose truth and not
error. Just as you wouldn't leave the health
area of their lives up to them, so you need to
be active in mentoring truth for them in the
spiritual area. You only have a short time to
do it, then they're grown and the shaping days
are over.

Secondly, maybe you're a parent and your
children are grown and gone, and perhaps
now you have grandchildren. Grandparents
are also models for their grandchildren. So it
matters to them what your spiritual status is
going to be.

Perhaps you're married but have no children yet, but plan to have them. It's so vital
that you take care of your spiritual status
BEFORE those children are born so there will

never be a question of what modeling you will do for them. Being raised in a Christian home will be the norm for them, and they won't have a chance to know anything else. Believe me, that's better than saying, "I'm going to be neutral and let my kids totally decide spiritual things on their own." Perhaps you're married, and in middle age or sunset years, and you never had any children of your own. You certainly owe it to your parents, who may even be dead and gone now, to be a believer in Jesus Christ. It is a legacy they perhaps passed down to you, and to not take it up is to greatly dishonor them, even though they may be gone.

The parents of Jesus saw to it that though He was the Son of God, He was trained in spiritual things. We really should do no less.

NINE

"I DON'T BELIEVE IN ORGANIZED RELIGION"

On a flight back to Seattle from Florida, I was sitting next to a young professional woman. She saw me with open Bible and a note pad, where I was putting the last minute touches on a sermon I would preach in only a few hours. She opened the conversation with, "Are you some kind of religious teacher?" When I assured her I was the pastor of a church in the Seattle area, she snapped back with a resolute sternness in her voice, "I don't believe in **organized** religion." The tone of voice was matter-of-fact, as if the issue were settled; but the fact that she initiated the conversation told me she really wanted a response from me. I didn't have to be prodded! I asked her, "I take it you've had some bad experiences with churches?" With a tone mixed between anger and disappointment she let me know she had had more than one bad experience. She told me that as a little girl she remembered seeing an old fashioned "church fight" in a meeting of her mother's congregation. She didn't even remember what the issue was, she just remembered hearing her mother say on the way home to whom she would be speaking and not speaking as a result of that disastrous congregational meeting. She also related to me that her one and only attempt to go to church in college happened to be on Stewardship Sunday, so she assumed all the church ever talked about was money. Her more recent attempt to go back to church revolved around a minister she really enjoyed hearing. He seemed so caring, so sincere, so powerful in his presentations. Then one Sunday an elder got up and announced he had been "released" due to immorality. That was it! "I was out of there, never to return...to that church or any church." She had written them all off. Having never accepted Christ, I could see why she was disillusioned. How easy it is to discredit the whole because of the rottenness of a part. She had three bad and bitter experiences with "organized" religion. By that she, and most others, mean the local church.

This young woman's appraisal of the local church reflects a gross misunderstanding of both the place the church has in Christianity, and what its make-up is all about.

First, let it be understood that the church is not some recent creation of man to help facilitate Christianity. It is divine in origin, and very much in the mind and will of God. While on earth, Jesus prophesied the coming of the church, claiming to be the builder Himself.

> "...on this rock I will build my church, and the gates of Hades will not overcome it." (Matthew 16:18b)

You don't have to be a theologian to know that Jesus said some phenomenal things about the church.

1. First, He will build the church, not man.

2. It will be built upon the **rock**. That rock is Christ Himself (I Corinthians 10:4).

3. It is **HIS** church, not man's. He said "my" church.

4. Hades (or hell itself) cannot overcome or over-power it.

This tells us that the church is indestructible, thus powerful.

To say "I don't believe in the organized church" is to say one doesn't believe in something for which Jesus built and empowered. It's also to say that you don't believe in something for which Jesus gave His life. We're told in Ephesians 5:25 that Jesus actually died for the church.

If it is important and valuable enough for Jesus to die for, we certainly can't say that we want no part of it.

The church is made up of the saved, not the perfect. The Bible tells us that the saved were added to the church. It is the repository of the saved (Acts 2:41). While it is made up of the saved, the saved are not perfect. They don't do everything right or say everything right. Their lack of perfection does not, however, invalidate the church.

If the founder of the church is Jesus Christ, the mission of the church is to make disciples. Before Jesus left this earth, He gave His last words in the form of a command to the church;

> "Therefore go and make disciples of all nations, baptizing them in the name of the Father and of the Son and of the Holy Spirit, and teaching them to obey everything I have commanded you." (Matthew 28:19-20a)

The church doesn't exist to "be" but to "do." It has a mission. It is ordained to be that divine/human organism through which the high and holy purpose of God is carried out in this world. So, the church not only has a right to exist, it has a lofty purpose which was given to it by the Lord.

When you read the book of Acts, you find the word "church" used extensively. The life of every believer centered itself in and around the church. It's important to know some truths about the church.

1. It's not humanly built, but divinely built.

2. It's not a building, but a people.

3. It's not an "organization," but an organism.

4. It's the place where true fellowship takes place.

5. It's the place where accountability takes place.

6. It's the place where corporate worship takes place.

7. It's the place where edification and service takes place.

8. It's the place from which missionaries are sent.

9. It's the place where communion and baptism are practiced.

10. It's the place where our spiritual gifts are to operate.

11. It's the place organized to show compassion when tragedy strikes.

We could go on, but the point is clear. The church has been divinely placed in this world for a purpose.

The fifth chapter of Ephesians tells us that the church is the bride of Christ. If it's true, that bride and groom are one, how can we be apart of the groom, and not be a part of the bride? Jesus loves the church. We're also told that the church is the body of Christ.

> "He is the head of the body, the church;" (Colossians 1:18)

Christ will return to this earth someday to escort His lovely bride out of this world and into heaven. He's coming back to get His church. At that time we will be either in the church or outside the church.

In the light of all this, it behooves us to speak well of the church, though in its human form it has blemishes.

To say we don't believe in the "organized" church implies we prefer perhaps the "disorganized" church. If the church is Biblically organized, we need not fear. The simple Biblical organization of the church is that Christ is the head of the church, and elders have been placed over each congregation to "direct the affairs of the church" (I Timothy 5:17). Members of the church are urged to be submissive to those leaders (Hebrews 13:17).

It's the role of those leaders to equip (perfect) all the other believers to do the work of the ministry.

In Ephesians 4, the Bible makes it clear God has appointed in the church apostles, prophets, evangelists, then pastors and teachers. These offices (people) exist, according to Ephesians 4:11ff to "prepare" God's people for works of service. Everything God has ever done has had a plan to it. The church is no exception. The head of the church is Christ. The foundation of the church is Christ, along with the apostles and prophets. The officers of the church, as stated, are listed for us. The "game plan" or purpose of the church is to go into all the world and make disciples. The financing of this project is to be by the voluntary contributions of its members (I Corinthians 16:1-2). The membership of the church is comprised of all the saved on earth. The ordinances of the church are baptism and the Lord's Supper.

In the light of all this, it's easy to see that the church exists in the world today as a design of God. It's not optional.

When someone says they don't want to accept Christ because they don't believe in the "organized" church, they are spurning the very organism that God created to contain His people while they're on the earth.

As long as the church is made up of **people** it will have flaws and imperfections. It won't always do everything right. It will occasionally fail to fulfill its purpose. It's leaders will also be flawed. From time to time, some will even fall into sin and bring disgrace on the Founder of the church.

But to say we don't want to belong to the organized church is to throw the baby out with the bath. It's like saying I want to serve my nation as a soldier, but I refuse to be in the army; I want to be a student and get an education, but I don't want to go to school; I want to live in Seattle, but I don't want to be a resident of Washington state.

The church on earth is far from a perfect institution. It can't be. "People" make up its membership! But it's still the church.

For the sake of where you will spend eternity, why not humble yourself, acknowledging that you are a sinner and can't save yourself, then throw yourself on the finished work of Christ and receive salvation. He will pardon your past, accept you, and place you in His church where He will protect you until the day He comes to take His church out of this world. It will be the smartest move you ever made!

"I'M JUST NOT READY YET"

All his buddies called him Red. In his mid-thirties, Red was a stocky man, with flaming red hair, a face that seemed to be flushed all the time, with tough-looking skin where the outside weather had obviously taken its toll. Red was a foreman with a mid-size construction company. I remember visiting him in their mobile home one cold, rainy evening. He was a tough-minded man, friendly, but definitely not willing to receive the Lord, though I had made the gospel presentation "alarmingly" clear! I knew he was nervous by my being in his home. He was newly married, and had taken on the responsibility of his wife's children. A new marriage, new family, new home, and now some new guy sitting in his house sharing the gospel with him because he had visited church. When we finally got around to the question; "Would you like to receive Jesus Christ right now?" his answer was in a low muffled voice; "I'm not ready yet." I came at it from another angle, but he kept answering, "I'm just not ready yet."

If you've read this far, maybe you are at the place where you're saying, "maybe someday in the future, but right now I'm not ready to say yes to Christ." If you are, let me ask you some very pointed questions;

1. Are You Not Ready to Acknowledge that You are a Sinner?

That's the first step. He who would be forgiven must first acknowledge that he NEEDS to be forgiven. The Bible says, "for all have sinned and fall short of the glory of God," (Romans 3:23). Are you not ready to admit that you are a sinner and thus have sin in your life?

2. Are You Not Ready to Receive God's Sure Cure for Sin?

The thing you're not ready to do is take a step that will cancel forever the guilt of your sin. If you went to a doctor for an examination, and he told you that a deadly leukemia was throughout your body and that if nothing is done, you have only three to six months to live, it would obviously not be good news. But while you're still in the examining room, suppose he says to you, "I have some good news...I have a serum which if taken, will cure your disease. Do you want it?" Would you say, "I'm not ready yet?"

Would you not be ready to receive a reprieve on your death penalty?

As we have seen, the consequences of sin means death—eternal separation from God for all of eternity. Receiving Jesus Christ as your Savior, however, cancels those consequences forever. Are you not ready for that?

Suppose you had fallen overboard without a life-jacket. You're thrashing around in the water, and drowning seems like a sure thing. Suddenly, a boat pulls up beside you just as you are ready to give up because you can't breathe anymore. Someone throws you a life preserver. Would you say, "I'm not ready yet!"? Of course you wouldn't. You would be ready to receive that life-preserver because of the gravity of the situation.

If I'm a sinner, and the wages of sin is death (both truths stand!), then the excuse of not being ready doesn't "hold water."

If you understand the imminent danger you're now in, then believe me, you're ready.

3. Are You Not Ready to Have the Condemnation and Curse Removed from Your Life?

We've already seen in previous chapters that because we're born sinners, we come into this world with an automatic condemnation resting over our lives. We've also seen that we're further cursed as we attempt to humanly remove that sin from our lives.

> "All who rely on the law are under a curse, for it is written: 'Cursed is everyone who does not

continue to do everything written in the Book of the Law.'" Galatians 3:10

Romans 8:1 tells us that the condemnation is removed once we're in Christ Jesus.

4. Are You Not Ready to Simply Trust the Finished Work of Christ?

Are you really NOT ready to yield all your striving and attempts to straighten your own life out over to Him, and accept what He did on the cross and at the tomb as God's price for your salvation?

5. Are You Really Not Ready to Begin a Full and Abundant Life, Knowing That You Will Have a Power and Strength You Never Had Before?

Not being ready to experience a new peace and joy found only in Christ, and not being ready to have the supernatural power of God within you to conquer all the problems life foists upon you is hard to understand.

6. Are You Really Not Ready to Become a Member of God's Forever Family?

When we receive Christ, we're adopted into God's vast family. We immediately become "related" to millions of fellow believers around the world. They become our new brothers and sisters in Christ, and we have a common parent, God. This family has rights and privileges we don't have while we're on the outside. The Bible makes it clear that before we accept Christ as our Savior, we belong to another family. Jesus talked about that family in John 8. The patriarch of that family of non-Christians is the devil. Jesus told the religious leaders, whose hearts were hard against Him, that they were acting just like their father, the devil. When you say you're not ready to receive Christ, you're really saying you're not ready to come into the most incredible inheritance whose worth no man can count. The Bible says we are "fellow heirs with Christ" (Romans 8:17). That means when we accept Christ, we come into all the wealth Jesus Christ owns. How much does

He own? All! Psalm 24 says that "the earth is the Lord's and everything in it." Psalm 50 tells us he "owns the cattle on a thousand hills." All the riches of all the universes are His. So to say, "I'm not ready to receive Christ right now" is to forfeit all that God has coming to you...in this life and the next!

7. Are You Really Not Ready to Receive Christ Within God's Window of Opportunity?

People who say, "I'm not ready yet" presume there will be a BETTER time for them to be ready. Necessarily, that time has to be in the future, since the past is gone and cannot be retrieved! That is not only a false presumption, but a very dangerous one.

God tells us that we have just a short window of opportunity in which to say yes to Christ.

> "Seek the Lord **WHILE** he may be found; call on Him **WHILE** he is near." (Isaiah 55:6)

The fact the word WHILE is in that sentence twice indicates a limited window of time. When is that time? It's **NOW**.

> "I tell you, now is the time of God's favor now is the day of salvation." (2 Corinthians 6:2b)

God's time is now. The past cannot be retrieved. The future is not promised. That leaves only one window of time...NOW!

There are three possible "events" after which it will be too late for you to receive Christ. The first one is your physical death. No matter how healthy you think you are, we're all one heartbeat away from eternity. You have nothing at all that will give you the certainty of life after you've reached the end of this page. The second "event" is the return of Jesus Christ to this world. The Bible says He's going to return; this time not to deal with sin, but to save those who are eagerly waiting for him. That's Christians.

It will be too late once He returns. He could come today! Every sign that needs to take place HAS taken place.

The third "event" is a line you're in danger of crossing, beyond which you become INCAPABLE of receiving Christ due to a hard heart. This comes by repeated rejections.

So, the truth is that you are ready. God is ready. Why not do it right now? What constitutes readiness? Need. You need the Lord...that makes you ready. If you received a phone call right now saying that a very wealthy relative died and left you an amount in excess of $50 million, and all you have to do is sign the papers of the executrix, would you say, "I'm just not ready"? I doubt it. The benefit is there, and you know how to write, so why would you wait? Remember, READINESS is predicated upon all conditions being in place for action. It's established that we're all sinners, and that sin has separated us from God (Isaiah 59:2). In His mercy, God has provided a cure (remedy) for our sin in having His Son Jesus Christ die on the cross, allowing His shed blood to be full payment for the penalty sin incurred. By accepting that offer, believing on Christ, trusting Him fully for salvation, the eternal benefits of that death on the cross, namely salvation, are transferred to us!

Something more valuable and more wonderful than $50 million awaits you. It's the priceless gift of eternal life in Christ. Why not receive it now? You are as ready as you can ever become right now! Why not pray this prayer and settle the issue for all eternity?

> Lord Jesus, I know I'm a sinner. I'm sorry for my sin. I believe You died on the cross for me, and paid my debt. I receive You now into my heart. Amen.

If you prayed that prayer and meant it, you are now ready to hear the Savior say to you; "Your sins are forgiven." You are also ready to go to heaven when you die. It doesn't get any better than that!

For you who prayed that prayer... welcome to the forever family of God! You're "family" now.

Oh, remember Red? Well, he accepted Christ within a few weeks. He's family now, too!

ELEVEN

JUST LOOK WHAT YOU'RE PROMISED!

No religion in the world even begins to claim to promise what Christianity promises. It can't. You have obviously read this far, and if you're willing to receive God's full and final offer you have a right to know exactly what His Word has promised you. It's called, "knowing your assets."

Just what are those assets?

1. The Forgiveness of All Sin

Please recall in earlier chapters that it is our sin that forms the barrier between us and God. Sin is like a "wedge" that separates us from God. Only through the removal of that sin can we have salvation. We've seen that sin cannot be removed by human effort, or humanly devised righteousness. Nor can they be removed by a volley of good works and deeds. All the "penance" in the world can't remove them. There is only one thing—the Blood of Christ, spilled on the cross by Jesus, the sacrificial lamb.

Nowhere is this promise of forgiveness clearer than in Acts.

> "All the prophets testify about him that everyone who believes in him receives forgiveness of sins through his name." (Acts 10:43)

But maybe you're thinking, "But I have committed some major, serious sins in my past. Can they all be forgiven?" YES!

> "...and the blood of Jesus, his Son, cleanses us from ALL sin." (I John 1:7b)

Forgiveness means we are released from the obligations that our sins created. Sin brings many things to us, but the worst obligation is death. The Bible says that "the wages of sin is death" (Romans 6:23). The "death" referred to here is not physical death, though all of us will experience that. It is a spiritual death, an eternal separation from God. Without God's forgiveness, that death can't be canceled.

Maybe you're wondering about the daily sins you commit once you have accepted Christ, how are they forgiven? The Bible has a clear answer for that.

> "If we confess our sins, he is faithful and just and will forgive us our sins and purify us from all unrighteousness." (I John 1:9)

Once you receive Jesus Christ by faith, He imparts your full forgiveness, once and for all.

2. The Presence of God's Holy Spirit in Your Life

No other religion in the world can make this claim. When we receive Christ, we are not asked to live the Christian life on our own. Before Jesus left this earth, He told His disciples that He would not leave them desolate.

"I will not leave you as orphans; I will come to you." (John 14:18)

Also;

"All this I have spoken while still with you. But the Counselor, the Holy Spirit, whom the Father will send in my name, will teach you all things and will remind you of everything I have said to you." (John 14:25-26)

When the very first gospel sermon was preached after the death, burial, resurrection, and ascension of Jesus, the Jews were told by Peter to repent and be baptized in the name of Jesus Christ. Upon their compliance with a changed heart, they were promised;

"...and you shall receive the gift of the Holy Spirit." (Acts 2:38)

That promise is a phenomenal promise, because of the ministry the Holy Spirit has in your life.

He does the following in you and for you:

a) He prods your memory on the teachings of Jesus (John 14:26).

b)   He guides us into all truth (John 16:13).

c)   He helps you pray correctly (Romans 8:26).

d)   He releases spiritual gifts in you so you can serve in the body of Christ, the church (I Corinthians 12:4-11).

e)   He serves as God's deposit, guaranteeing our salvation (Ephesians 1:13).

f)   He produces good fruit in our lives (Galatians 5:22ff).

g)   He continuously sanctifies us (II Thessalonians 2:13).

h)   He testifies with our spirit that we're children of God (Romans 8:16).

i)   He empowers us to witness (Acts 1:8).

The Holy Spirit takes up residence in us when we believe on Jesus and receive Him as our Savior. He never leaves us, but continues as our divine companion, not only guiding us, but protecting us.

3. A Full and Abundant Life Here and Now

Many think the CHIEF benefit of being a Christian has to do with the future life only.

Not so. Jesus promised a quality of life unparalleled.

> "I have come that they may have life and have
> it to the full." (John 10:10)

What was the "life" to which Jesus referred? It certainly wasn't just physical life. Those to whom He spoke had that, or they wouldn't be hearing him! He wasn't referring to everlasting life, because everyone already has that...either life unending in heaven or in hell. So he was obviously referring to a depth and quality of life He brings that can be had no place else and given by no one else.

Years later, Paul summed it up in these words;

> "...and you have been given fullness in
> Christ,..."(Colossians 2:10)

That can only mean one thing. Other things may enhance our lives such as money, health, fame, proper esteem, etc., but life never reaches its fullness until we have received Jesus Christ as Savior and Lord. Then, and only then can we reach "fullness."

What does that "full" life have here and now that can't be had without Christ?

a) PEACE!

I'm told that certain drugs like valium can effect a calmness and peace. Those involved in Yoga and Transcendental Meditation claim they derive a certain peace from their exercises. Drinkers claim a couple of drinks after a stressful day can calm them down and bring some semblance of peace. But make no mistake about it, the peace Jesus brings has two characteristics these other things don't have. First, its source is divine and, secondly, it lasts!

> "Peace I leave with you; my peace I give to you. I do not give to you as the world gives. Do not let your hearts be troubledand do not be afraid." (John 14:27)

Also, in Colossians 3:15 the Bible talks about the peace of Christ RULING in our hearts. When tragedy strikes, grief comes, disease invades, or financial loss attacks, the believer in Christ has a resource of peace to fall back on that is unique and effective. We further have the promise from the Bible that peace stands like a sentinel to protect our tender hearts.

> "And the peace of God which transcends all understanding, will guard your hearts and your minds in Christ Jesus." (Philippians 4:7)

b) JOY!

This abundant, full life here and now is also marked by joy. It is a joy that deeply differs from this world's passing spurts of jaded happiness. Jesus said;

> "I have told you this so that my joy may be in you and that your joy may be complete."
> (John 15:11)

The word "complete" means full, over-flowing. He's talking about that inner seren-ity and sense of well-being that is yours re-gardless of what the outer circumstances may be dishing up.

c) WORRY-FREE LIFE

Maybe the most wonderful characteristic of the abundant life we have in Christ here and now is a life free of worry and anxiety.

> "Do not be anxious about anything, but in everything, by prayer and petition, with thanksgiving, present your requests to God." (Philippians 4:6)

None of this is to say that the Christian is to have no concerns. Of course, we have them. But there is a fine line where concern gives over to worry, and from the Sermon on the Mount clear through the book of Revelation, we're taught that once we're saved, we never have to worry about anything again.

This list could well go on and on and on. In Him we have forgiveness of our past and present, we have the gift of His Holy Spirit, constantly present, and we have abundant, full life. There is another privilege that often goes unmentioned.

d) PRAYER!

Volumes have been penned about the power and blessing of prayer. People outside of Jesus Christ do not have this privilege—it's open only to the believer—and what a privilege!! Jesus gave us a model prayer in Matthew 6 that covers all the bases.

"*Our Father*" assures us of our unique relationship to God...He is our heavenly parent.

"*Who art in heaven*" tells us that God is wholly other—that He is a spiritual being, not an earthly being.

"*Hallowed be thy name*" tells me that I'm to revere His name, and remember that it is a holy name.

"*Thy Kingdom Come, Thy Will be done, on earth as it is in heaven.*" This tells me I'm to pray for conditions to exist on earth as they do in heaven. They don't now, because man is sinful, but it does give me the focus of that prayer.

It means I desire God's will to be done as perfectly on earth as it's done in heaven. In heaven, it's done perfectly, no flaws, no hitches.

"*Give us this day our daily bread*" means that prayer is the way God wants me to let Him know I'm depending on Him for sustenance. God intended prayer to be the communication channel by which we make contact with Him.

"*Forgive us our debts as we forgive our debtors.*" It's in prayer that confession for sin is made. Though His blood constantly cleanses us from sin, God has ordained prayer as the place where we are to confess those sins to Him.

"*Lead us not into temptation, but deliver us from evil.*" It's in prayer that we find power to win over temptation, and find protection from the evil one.

"*For thine is the greatness, and the power, and the glory for ever and ever.*" This is the praise part of prayer. All prayer must start with praising God, worshipping Him in the splendor of His holiness.

e) ETERNAL LIFE!

It may be the last to mention, but it certainly isn't the least. In John 14 Jesus made it clear that He was going to prepare a place for His people to live forever. It's called Heaven. Revelation 21 give us a vivid description, though words fail to really describe its splendor. Perhaps the greatest promise in the whole Bible is John 3:16;

> "For God so loved the world that he gave his one and only son, that whoever believes in him shall not perish but have eternal life." (John 3:16)

The sequence is BELIEVING, then RECEIVING. John also wrote in his first epistle;

> "And this is the testimony: God has given us eternal life, and this life is in his Son." (I John 5:11)

One thing many believers tend to forget. Eternal life is not just something future, we have it right now in the present tense.

> "I tell you the truth, he who believe HAS eternal life." (John 6:47)

That's here and now. That's present tense. While we possess it now, it will change forms someday when we die physically.

At that time, we will all enter heaven, there will be a new environment, a new atmosphere, and we'll have a new body that will match those things.

> "Now we know that if the earthly tent we live in is destroyed, we have a building from God, an eternal house in heaven, not built by human hands." (II Corinthians 5:1)

Paul likens your body to a tent. Tents are never permanent dwelling places. Soldiers bunk down in them temporarily while in battle. Campers use them for a week-end camping trip. They seldom last very long. They fade, they rot, they tear, they leak. Paul really used a graphic metaphor when he described this human body of ours. It's so temporary! The older it gets the more faded and dilapidated it becomes. Paul says that for the Christian, the day will come when we will lay aside the tent. It can no longer house us. As I write this chapter, I was interrupted by a phone call to say that one of our very closest friends just died of cancer. She was 55. She's struggled with that disease for almost two years. It ravaged her body to the end. Though I'm sad and will miss her, I feel a swelling sense of joy for her. She's got a new body as of 3:30 this morning! She's in heaven, the place she often talked about and anticipated. She's probably sad for us who have to still watch our tents wear out.

You may be asking, "All that sounds fine, but what if we lose that eternal life before we die?" The Bible teaches that we will never lose it, and that Jesus will never let us go.

> "All that the Father gives me will come to me, and whoever comes to me I will never drive away." (John 6:37)

What a promise! He will never shut us out, reject us, turn us away, or throw us out. Jesus further assures us that not only will He not reject us, now one else can pull us away from eternal life.

> "I give them eternal life, and they shall never perish; no one can snatch them out of my hand." (John 10:28)

Couple this with the fact that Peter, in his epistle, says that we have an inheritance given to us—which, by the way, is the gift of eternal life—and that inheritance will never PERISH, SPOIL or FADE. I would call that permanent.

If you have read this far, and are still not a Christian, I beseech you, give your heart to Christ right now! Don't put this off. Don't defer it to another time, or relegate it to a position of unimportance.

Twenty-five years ago, I heard a Persian fable which contains a principle that is no fable.

Once there was a Persian king who had great wealth and good looks. He feasted on anything he wanted, and his money could almost buy the world! But in spite of all this, the king was depressed, and very sad most of the time. To cheer him, he hired a jester whose antics and clowning made him laugh. The king was taken with the court fool, and one day gave him a white stick saying, "When you find a bigger fool than yourself, give him this stick."

One day the king became seriously ill, and he was afraid. His illness became critical, and he lay dying.

To cheer him, he called his court jester to make him laugh one more time. When the jester came to the king's bedside, he asked the king, "And where is the king going?" "On a very long journey," the king responded. "Hast thou made preparations for the journey?" the jester asked. "No," replied the king, "I have made no preparations." Reaching inside his cloak, the jester pulled out the white stick the king had given him years earlier. Handing it to the king on his death bed, the jester said, "I only trifle with the things of time, but you have trifled with the things of eternity. You're a bigger fool than I."

It may be a fable, but its truth is real. Only one thing matters when you're facing the grim reaper—when you're staring death in the face. Are you ready for the journey? If you're not, why not repeat this prayer right now?

Dear God...I know I'm a sinner...I'm truly sorry for my sin...Lord Jesus, I believe You died on the cross for me, and rose again. Come into my heart right now...I accept You as my personal Savior. In Jesus' name, Amen.

Well, did you pray that? If so, WELCOME TO GOD'S FOREVER FAMILY!

CONSIDER THESE TESTIMONIES

When the woman of Samaria met Jesus and accepted Him as her Savior and Messiah, she went back into the city a changed woman. Her testimony was simple;

> "Come, see a man who told me everything I ever did." (John 4:29)

Many in that city came to know Christ as a result of her testimony.

When Jesus healed a man who had been blind from birth, the man was questioned by his neighbors and religious officials. His simple testimony was;

> "One thing I do know. I was blind but now I see." (John 9:25b)

But these New Testament testimonies aren't the only ones. Millions of people since then have "made the plunge" and thanked God the rest of their lives. In church history, men like Paul, Ambrose, Cyprian, St.Augustine, Martin Luther and John Knox made this decison. Also, Billy Sunday, D.L. Moody, Jonathan Edwards, Billy Graham, Chuck Colson, Glenn Campbell, Pat Boone, A.C. Green, Jim Zorn, Dave Dravecky, Steve Largent, and hundreds more well knowns have made the great decison. where does the list ever end? These names I've mentioned are almost household words because of their public lives. So what about the plain old "Joes" who aren't known to the public?

Here are but a few of the people I've had the humble joy and privilege of being used as a small cog in their conversion. For their privacy, I'll change their names, but their stories are true!

Ted was an insurance agent who had a profitable company. Raised in a religious home, he sowed his wild oats in his late teens and early twenties. He married, had two

children, and his wife became a Christian. She
eagerly prayed and prayed for him. People
shared with him again and again, but he held
out. He was climbing the corporate ladder
rather rapidly, when he agreed to attend our
church with his wife. The more he attended
and heard the gospel appeal, the softer he
became. Then one Easter Sunday morning, he
came under a heavy conviction at the close of
the service and came forward to receive Christ,
weeping uncontrollably. I had a very, very
small part in that whole process by preaching
a sermon that day about Christ's sufficiency
to save and keep us. In Ted's words, "My
whole life turned around at that point, and I
knew I had been miraculously changed."
That was over fifteen years ago, and Ted is
still going strong for the Lord.

Don's was a different story altogether. He
was a rough and gruff construction foreman.
He had done it all, said it all, and was recently
divorced from his wife. His life was one big
mess. He was in debt, in depression, and
terribly angry. He was invited to church by
one of his men, and came only because he was

desperate. I went to see him in his home where he was living with his girlfriend who, interestingly enough, had recently received the Lord but was not yet mature enough to move out. As I shared the gospel with him, he was terribly resistent, but it was the kind of resistence that was fighting the convicting power of the Holy Spirit.

I was relentless with Don. Finally, after I had answered every argument he raised, he threw his hands up and shouted, "All right, all right! I'll accept Christ, but it better work." I assured him Jesus never fails. When we stood after kneeling to pray the believer's prayer, Don's face glowed. I saw a smile I had never seen in my life. He quit his fowl language, his violence, his drinking, and his anger and depression left him almost immediately. Don later became responsible for leading scores of hardened men to Jesus Christ. His words, "I never really lived till I accepted Jesus Christ as Savior," were echoed hundreds of times as, in his own crude way, he shared his personal testimony with other men.

And then there was Ben. I first met Ben when he was 91, living in a retirement home. Witty, set in his ways, Ben related to me his life's history. He told of being an electrical inspector in his home state, but in all of his 91 years, no one had ever approached him about Christianity.

I had the privilege of sharing the gospel with him, and watched as he invited Christ into his heart. I also had the joy of watching him be lowered in the watery grave of baptism. In Ben's words, "I wish I had found this about 75 years ago!" What a testimony!

One last miraculous testimony is in order. A man I knew all my life to be a mean, beligerent, and spiteful person went on my prayer list for salvation early. For ever twenty years I prayed for his salvation. An alcoholic, this man dealt misery to his wife and three children. Finally, his drinking and violence became so unbearable he was divorced. The drinking continued, along with two packs of cigarettes a day. I received a phone call that he was having heart surgery because of a severe heart attack. I rushed to his bedside only a few

hours after they brought him from Coronary
Care, where he had stayed a whole day longer
because of severe complications. They almost
lost him once on the table, and then again in
recovery. Bending over him with tubes, valves,
pumps, and oxygen all attached to his body,
I again shared the gospel with him. He repeated the prayer of acceptance after me,
finally, after all these years of praying and
pleading. Today, he's retired, but attends
church, reads his Bible, goes to weekly Bible
study, and no longer drinks, smokes, and has
no trace of violence in his life. Why? In his
words, "The Lord performed a surgery on my
soul that was more important than the surgery on my physical heart, and I'm a new
man." That man happens to be my blood
brother, Charles. If God can change his life,
and can change my life, then God can change
your life. All He needs is your surrender.

Maybe this is all new to you, and there is
a lot you just don't know. The truth is, you
don't need to know a lot of things, just a few.

1. You need to know that you are a
sinner, separated from God (Romans 3:23).

2. You need to know that you can't save yourself (Psalm 49:7).

3. Jesus Christ died on the cross for you and paid the penalty for your sins (I Corinthians 15:3).

4. You can be saved if you will believe and confess Jesus to be your Lord (Romans 10:9,10).

Sounds too simple? While accepting Christ has profound and eternal implications, the process is really quite simple. It doesn't require a lot of Bible knowledge, nor does it demand you have a thoroughly worked out "theology." The Bible teaches that "...faith comes from hearing the message, and the message is heard through the word of Christ."(Romans 10:17)

Why not reach out right now and receive the free gift of salvation God wants to give you? Receive it like a child receives sustenance from its parent. You've tried the present way, and it hasn't worked. Remember, you have nothing to lose but the guilt of your sins, and an eternity in hell without God! That's a good loss! Will you pray this prayer right now?

Dear God, I confess that I'm a sinner, and I can't do anything to change my status. I believe that Jesus died on the cross and rose again for me. Lord Jesus, I receive You right now into my life. I commit all of me that I know how to all of You that I understand, I welcome you into my life to do with me whatever You desire. I freely receive the gift of salvation. In Jesus' name, Amen.

If you prayed that prayer, or the prayer after any of the other chapters, please write to me and let me know:

Dr. Bob Moorehead
9051-132nd Ave. N.E.
Kirkland, WA 98033

For additional copies of this book:
Overlake Christian Bookstore
(206) 828-7270
1-800-929-4413